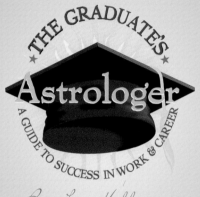

THE GRADUATE'S
Astrologer
A GUIDE TO SUCCESS IN WORK & CAREER

By Lee Holloway

**Andrews McMeel
Publishing**

Kansas City

The Graduate's Astrologer:
A Guide to Success in Work & Career
Text, design, and compilation
© 2000 Lionheart Books, Ltd.

The Graduate's Astrologer:
A Guide to Success in Work & Career
was produced by Lionheart Books, Ltd.
Atlanta, GA 30341

Design: Carley Wilson Brown

Andrews McMeel Publishing,
an Andrews McMeel Universal company,
4520 Main Street, Kansas City, Missouri 64111.

ISBN:0-7407-1093-1
Library of Congress Catalog Card Number:
00-106947

~~~~~~~~~~~~~~~~~~~~~~~~~~~~~~

Contents

~~~~~~~~~~~~~~~~~~~~~~~~

Should you be a rock star or an actor with your name in lights, a pilot or an astronaut circling the globe in flight? A fashion designer, captain of industry, or a judge on the bench, or would being a chef or an author make sense? Is Aries a natural at leading the way, and would Virgo do best by avoiding the fray?

Will Shakespeare once penned the famous phrase "To be or not to be," but perhaps a more apt question is *to be what*? In today's world of exploding technology and rapid changes, achieving success in your job and career can seem like *Mission Impossible*. This book can give you an astrological advantage when making one of life's most important choices by tapping into your sign's special talents and passions. It can help you achieve your dreams and desires and reach the pot of gold at the end of the rainbow *through the magic that lies within you*.

As you read this guidebook to success in your work and career, remember "If you *love* what you do, you'll never *work* a day in your life." May you live long, laugh often, and prosper in all you do.

Your Graduate's Astrologer

Lee Holloway

Aries

...on the Road to Success

Faster than a speeding bullet and able to leap tall buildings in a single bound . . . . Well, Aries, you may not *quite* be a Superman or Superwoman, but you don't miss by much. With your initiative, courage, love of a challenge, and innate skills for success you could write the book that sets the standards for others to follow. Your leadership and decisiveness are

"To be a success in business, be daring,
be first, be different." ~ *Marchant*

Element: Fire
Quality: Cardinal
Ruler: Mars
Symbol: Ram

Aries
COMPATIBLE
SIGNS

~*Fire Signs*
★ Aries
★ Leo
★ Sagittarius

~*Air Signs*
★ Gemini
★ Libra
★ Aquarius

also winning qualities and the only problem you might have is reining in your impulsiveness, enthusiasm, and impatience at times.

Once you've set your "eyes on the prize," your enterprising skills enable you to come up with innovative ways to achieve your goals, which is why you're often found at the head of a company, project, or department. Independent, pioneering, creative, and direct, you're a formidable competitor in any field you choose. *Your magic lies in your ability to dare and do, and to lead the way.* Consider the success of talented Aries like Gloria Steinem, Eric Clapton, and Leonardo da Vinci, trailblazers who dared to break new ground in their chosen fields. *Freedom* and *independence* are *key to your success and happiness*, because you need room to expand and *explore* your diverse talents and creativity.

CAPTURES THE

Aries PHILOSOPHY:

"Leadership is *action*, not position."
~ *Donald H. McGannon*

~~~~~~~~~~~~~~~~~~~~~

Successful Aries

Al Gore, Maya
Angelou, David E. Kelley,
Rosie O'Donnell, Mariah
Carey, Andrew Lloyd Webber,
Scott Turow, Alec Baldwin, Celine
Dion, Diana Ross, Steven Tyler,
Sarah Jessica Parker, Elton
John, Aretha Franklin,
Marlon Brando, Johann
Sebastian Bach

Preferred Professions

Director,
Surgeon, Racer, Engineer,
Stunt Person, Graphologist,
Barber, Butcher, Pitcher, Explorer,
Receptionist, Steel Worker,
Military Officer, Firefighter,
Bill Collector, Arms
Manufacturer,
Welder

Taurus

...on the Road to Success

I t's been said that "slow and steady wins the race," and that's especially true for you, Taurus. With your *uncommon* common sense, you know patience is a virtue and a *necessity* to build a life that is secure as well as rewarding. Your love of security and the good things in life is the incentive to make you work as long as needed to get what you want.

14

"Our patience will achieve more than
our force." ~ *Edmond Burke*

Element: Earth
Quality: Fixed
Ruler: Venus
Symbol: Bull

Taurean
COMPATIBLE
SIGNS

~*Earth Signs*
★ Taurus
★ Virgo
★ Capricorn

~*Water Signs*
★ Cancer
★ Scorpio
★ Pisces

Venus, your ruler, bestows friendliness and creativity, qualities that hasten your progress and make you an asset for any company or venture. Your affability and methodical approach can also make you an effective manager. As an earth sign you're as solid as a rock and a force to be reckoned with when you focus your talents toward your goals and desires. Barbra Streisand, George Lucas, and William Shakespeare are a few examples of the varied talents Taureans possess *and their ability to create works that stand the test of time.*

Your magic lies in living in the moment and dealing with life practically. Others will rely on that "down to earth" quality because they sense you have your head on straight and your feet on the ground, marvelous qualities in today's fast-paced, who-know-what's-next world.

CAPTURES THE

Taurean PHILOSOPHY:

"All things come to him who waits."
~ *Longfellow*

✕ ✕ ✕ ✕ ✕ ✕ ✕ ✕ ✕ ✕ ✕ ✕ ✕ ✕ ✕ ✕ ✕ ✕ ✕

Successful Taureans

Enrique Iglesias,
Michelle Pfeiffer, Bono,
Cate Blanchett, Andre Agassi,
Cher, Billy Joel, Enya, Jerry
Seinfeld, Freud, Audrey Hepburn,
Jack Nicholson, Nora Ephron,
Mike Wallace, Pierce Brosnan,
Jay Leno, Stevie Wonder,
Gabriel Byrne

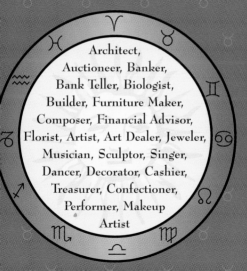

Preferred Professions

Architect, Auctioneer, Banker, Bank Teller, Biologist, Builder, Furniture Maker, Composer, Financial Advisor, Florist, Artist, Art Dealer, Jeweler, Musician, Sculptor, Singer, Dancer, Decorator, Cashier, Treasurer, Confectioner, Performer, Makeup Artist

Gemini
...on the Road to Success

How do you capture a butterfly without damaging its wings?" is the question when considering Gemini's talents, temperament, and career prospects. Think of quicksilver or the lightning speed of a hummingbird's wings and you begin to get an image of a Gemini's quick and restless nature. Thanks to Mercury, your ruler, you're as high-strung as a racehorse,

"Variety's the very spice of life that gives it
all its flavor." ~*William Cowper*

Element: Air
Quality: Mutable
Ruler: Mercury
Symbol: Twins

Gemini
COMPATIBLE
SIGNS

~*Air Signs*
★ Gemini
★ Libra
★ Aquarius
~*Fire Signs*
★ Aries
★ Leo
★ Sagittarius

as inventive and imaginative as they come, with an innate curiosity, wit, and a youthful exuberance. Successful Geminis like Mike Myers, Jewel, and Paul McCartney personify some of the diverse talents in this sign. *And like the butterfly,* you do best when you have as much freedom and variety as possible.

To be happy *and* successful in your work and career, Gemini, you need mental stimulation, variety, *and* the chance to experiment and explore. If you consider your restless temperament when making your choices you'll avoid the Gemini pitfall of frequent job changes and scattering your energy and effectiveness.

Your magic lies in your intellect, adaptability, and curiosity and should be used to communicate your novel ideas, solutions, and perspectives to others. In a humdrum world of routines you're like a breath of fresh air in springtime, Gemini.

CAPTURES THE

Gemini PHILOSOPHY:

"Fortune is full of fresh variety."
~ *Richard Barnfield*

Successful Geminis

Annette Bening, Donald Trump, Brooke Shields, Melissa Etheridge, John F. Kennedy, Alanis Morissette, Gauguin, Nicole Kidman, Johnny Depp, Marilyn Monroe, Bob Dylan, Judy Garland, Drew Carey, Courtney Cox, Kenny G, Steffi Graf

Preferred Professions

Writer,
Literary Critic,
Newspaper Publisher,
Librarian, Executive, Editor,
Speaker, Teacher, Typesetter,
Clerical Worker, Auto Mechanic,
News Commentator, Playwright,
Respiratory Therapist, Reporter,
Weather Forecaster,
Spokesperson, Printer,
Linguist

Cancer
...on the Road to Success

Your sensitive, emotional, Cancer nature might seem unsuited for dealing with the stress and competition that often accompanies success, but nothing could be farther from the truth. You are one of the most resilient signs in the zodiac and can proudly boast that many financially successful people are born under this sign. Though sensitive,

"All great discoveries are made
by men whose feelings run ahead of their
thinking." ~ *C.H. Parkhurst*

Element: Water
Quality: Cardinal
Ruler: Moon
Symbol: Crab

Cancer
COMPATIBLE
SIGNS

~*Water Signs*
★ Cancer
★ Scorpio
★ Pisces

~*Earth Signs*
★ Taurus
★ Virgo
★ Capricorn

you have drive and initiative to spare, along with instincts and intuition that border on the prophetic. These are considerable assets for success in any career, as well as a key ingredient for your personal happiness.

Cancers like Armani, Tom Hanks, and Robin Williams illustrate the range of talents and career options available to you. *Your magic lies in your depth of feeling and your sensitivity.* You can express your feelings in a variety of ways, like Rembrandt with an artist's palette or as an actor, a writer, or in any job or profession that captures your heart and interest. Your feelings are a major part of your makeup so pay attention to them when choosing your work or career. Your tender heart and nature, though resilient, will flourish *best* in a work environment that feels "like a home away from home."

CAPTURES THE

Cancer PHILOSOPHY:

"To feel fully is to live fully."
~ *Dr. David Viscott*

~~~~~~~~~~~~~~~~~~~~~~~~~~~~~~~~~

Successful Cancers

Harrison Ford, Liv Tyler, Tom Cruise, Meryl Streep, Carlos Santana, Michelle Kwan, Chris Isaak, Armani, Bill Cosby, Isabelle Adjani, Princess Diana, Thoreau, Vera Wang, Danny Glover, Hemingway, Mary Stuart Masterson

Preferred Professions

Producer,
Antique Dealer, Historian,
Caterer, Archivist, Chef,
Genealogist, Obstetrician,
Teacher, Museum Curator, Realtor,
Restaurateur, Microbiologist,
Oceanographer, Seaman,
Silversmith, Plumber,
Wholesaler, Landowner,
Fisherman

Leo
. . . on the Road to Success

JULY 24 ~ AUGUST 23

As the only sign in the zodiac ruled by the Sun, you're in a class all your own, Leo. Your sunny personality and dignity are gifts of your solar birthright along with a few others like generosity, creativity, leadership, and a great heart, so, when you're utilizing those assets, you're hard to beat.

A born leader with a dramatic flair,

``All the world's a stage and all the men and omen are merely players.'' ~ *Shakespeare*

Element: Fire
Quality: Fixed
Ruler: Sun
Symbol: Lion

Leo
COMPATIBLE
SIGNS

↝ *Fire Signs*
★ Aries
★ Leo
★ Sagittarius

↝ *Air Signs*
★ Gemini
★ Libra
★ Aquarius

your style will show in any work or career you choose. Madonna, Martha Stewart, Jacqueline Kennedy, and Robert Redford exemplify some of the distinctive talents and styles Leos possess and have used to attain success. You can excel at many things if you don't limit your scope or imagination and decide what captures your heart and interest. Feeling a sense of pride and loving what you do is vital to your happiness.

Your magic lies in your

loving heart and generous nature, which you often use to help others develop their talents and creativity. You can be a shining example of leadership with humility and integrity. Your dignity and confidence gain trust, while your liberal praise brings out the best in others. Is it any wonder that Leo is often so successful and admired by so many?

CAPTURES THE
Leo's PHILOSOPHY:

"A life or career without heart is meaningless." ~ *Anonymous*

~~~~~~~~~~~~~~~~~~~~~

Successful Leos

Bill Clinton, Angela Bassett, Steve Case, Tori Amos, Steve Wozniak, Sandra Bullock, Antonio Banderas, Halle Barry, Martin Sheen, Debra Messing, Pete Sampras, Neil Armstrong, Carl Jung, Charlize Theron, Kevin Spacey, Melanie Griffith

Preferred Professions

Actor, Artist, Athlete, Entrepreneur, Cardiologist, Comedian, Film Director/Producer, Stockbroker, Teacher, Jeweler, Theatrical Agent, Obstetrician, Goldsmith, Promoter, Emcee, Patron of the Arts, Nightclub Performer, Speculator

Virgo

...on the Road to Success

AUGUST 24 ~ SEPTEMBER 22

Your reputation as one of the most tireless workers in the zodiac is well deserved. Your need to be active, useful, and perfect as possible comes from your Virgo sign, while Mercury, your ruler, bestows you with precision, efficiency, abundant nervous energy, and curiosity. You're the best at what you do because you're task-oriented, blessed with

"Have a place for everything, and have
everything in its place." ~ *Anonymous*

Element: Earth
Quality: Mutable
Ruler: Mercury
Symbol: Virgin

Virgo
COMPATIBLE
SIGNS

~*Earth Signs*
★ Taurus
★ Virgo
★ Capricorn

~*Water Signs*
★ Cancer
★ Scorpio
★ Pisces

practicality and good judgment.

Is it any wonder your workload is usually overflowing? Your varied skills, proficiency, and responsible nature make you a valued asset to any company, venture, or project. Your self-confidence increases with age and could be hastened by giving yourself credit when due to offset your perfectionism and high standards. Virgos Andrea Bocelli, Sean Connery, and Shania Twain show the range of talent available to your nothing-but-the-best-will-do birth sign and how that trait translates to success.

Your magic lies in your reason, practicality, and efficiency. Your ability to find the right words and the most efficient way to do things makes you a desirable manager or staff member in a wide range of jobs or professions. While your need for perfection may be the bane of your existence, it's like manna from heaven for the rest of us who benefit from it.

CAPTURES THE

Virgo PHILOSOPHY:

"Trifles make perfection, and perfection is no trifle." ~ *Michelangelo*

Successful Virgos

Stephen King, LeAnn Rimes, Regis Philbin, Faith Hill, H. G. Wells, Claudia Schiffer, Scott Hamilton, Richard Gere, Cameron Diaz, Marc Anthony, Gloria Estefan, Goran Visnjic, Raquel Welch, Harry Connick, Jr., Agatha Christie, Peter Sellers

Preferred Professions

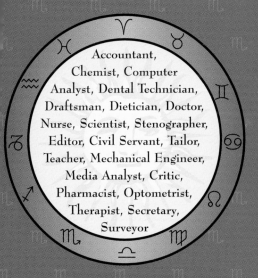

Accountant, Chemist, Computer Analyst, Dental Technician, Draftsman, Dietician, Doctor, Nurse, Scientist, Stenographer, Editor, Civil Servant, Tailor, Teacher, Mechanical Engineer, Media Analyst, Critic, Pharmacist, Optometrist, Therapist, Secretary, Surveyor

Libra

...on the Road to Success

In a world where beauty and charm are "the coin of the realm," you've got money to spare. Whether your beauty radiates from within or without is merely a question of form, not substance, and is the tip of the iceberg when compared to your talents. Your eye for form and love of balance and harmony is as welcome in business and law as it is in the arts, while your pleasing personality, diplomacy, and

"That action alone is just that does not harm either party to a dispute." ~ *Gandhi*

Element: Air
Quality: Cardinal
Ruler: Venus
Symbol: Scales

Libra
COMPATIBLE
SIGNS

~*Air Signs*
★ Gemini
★ Libra
★ Aquarius

~*Fire Signs*
★ Aries
★ Leo
★ Sagittarius

tact allow you to excel in areas ranging from politics to public relations. Successful Librans like Johnny Carson, Gwyneth Paltrow, Michael Crichton, and Sting illustrate the varieties of work and careers available for those born with the winning qualities of this sign.

Your sense of fair play, justice, and equality may cause you consternation at times when making a decision, but that's a small price to pay for the abundant gifts bestowed to you by Venus, your benevolent ruler. *Your magic lies in your love of justice, balance, and harmony . . .* You are the peacemaker, gifted with grace, charm, and beauty, and you possess some of the best qualities found in the human heart. Where wouldn't your qualities and skills be wanted in today's world?

CAPTURES THE

Libra PHILOSOPHY:

"Beauty in things exists in the mind that contemplates them." ~ *David Hume*

47

Successful Libras

Catherine Zeta-Jones, Matt Damon, Jimmy Carter, Mira Sorvino, Will Smith, Sigourney Weaver, Mahatma Gandhi, Paul Simon, Anne Rice, Susan Sarandon, Sting, Verdi, Kate Winslet, Ralph Lauren, Elisabeth Shue, Jackson Browne, Toni Braxton

Preferred Professions

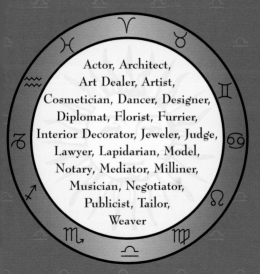

Actor, Architect,
Art Dealer, Artist,
Cosmetician, Dancer, Designer,
Diplomat, Florist, Furrier,
Interior Decorator, Jeweler, Judge,
Lawyer, Lapidarian, Model,
Notary, Mediator, Milliner,
Musician, Negotiator,
Publicist, Tailor,
Weaver

Scorpio

...on the Road to Success

OCTOBER 23 ~ NOVEMBER 21

All or nothing at all" is a song Frank Sinatra turned into a classic, but it could have been written for Scorpio. That single phrase sums up your approach to life, personally and professionally, since you do nothing by halves. You're blessed with a shrewd understanding of people and business, so trust your instincts and follow your passion. A life

"To burn with this hard, gemlike flame, to
maintain this ecstasy, is success in life."
~ *Walter Pater*

Element: Water
Quality: Fixed
Ruler: Pluto
Symbol: Scorpion

Scorpio
COMPATIBLE
SIGNS

~ *Water Signs*
★ Cancer
★ Scorpio
★ Pisces

~ *Earth Signs*
★ Taurus
★ Virgo
★ Capricorn

without passion is a gray life for your intense, sometimes obsessive nature, Scorpio, and it stems from Pluto, your powerful ruler. With your attention riveted on what you want, you can galvanize all your energy and assets to attain your goals or desires.

Your magic lies in your passionate intensity and acute perceptions, and can be used in any area you choose. Pluto, the ruler of Scorpio *and* atomic energy, is the potent source of your passion, and why your all-or-nothing nature won't settle for less than you desire. Scorpio: you were built to face reality, not superficiality. You're meant to scale the heights and plumb the depths and nothing less will fulfill you. It's easy to see why Scorpios like Bill Gates, Ted Turner, Jonas Salk, and Rodin exemplify the focus, intensity, passion, and power inherent in this sign.

CAPTURES THE

Scorpio PHILOSOPHY:

"The desire accomplished is sweet to the soul." ~ *Proverbs 19*

Successful Scorpios

Hillary Rodham Clinton, Leonardo DiCaprio, Calista Flockhart, Calvin Klein, Jodie Foster, Julia Roberts, Meg Ryan, Matthew McConaughey, Winona Ryder, Demi Moore, Dylan McDermott, Bo Derek, Robert Kennedy, Maria Shriver, Bonnie Raitt, Kevin Kline

Preferred Professions

Psychiatrist, Psychologist, Insurance Broker, Surgeon, Coroner, Archaeologist, Chemist, Tax Collector, Secret Service Agent, Dentist, Estate Lawyer, Credit Manager, Lab Technician, Pharmacist, Policeman, Demolition Expert, Brewer, Counselor

Sagittarius
...on the Road to Success

NOVEMBER 22 ~ DECEMBER 21

T he time has come,'" the Walrus said, / 'To talk of many things: / Of shoes—and ships—and sealing-wax—/ Of cabbages—and kings—'" aptly describe the range of interest and intellect bestowed on lucky Sagittarius. With excellent communication skills, you are as at ease in the pulpit as in the role of a jester, as profound as a mystic or as childlike as Peter Pan.

"Success is a journey, not a destination."
~ *Ben Sweetland*

Element: Fire
Quality: Mutable
Ruler: Jupiter
Symbol: Archer

Sagittarius
COMPATIBLE
SIGNS

~*Fire Signs*
★ Aries
★ Leo
★ Sagittarius

~*Air Signs*
★ Gemini
★ Libra
★ Aquarius

Your magic lies in your belief in life, your inherent faith and optimism that the force that lit the heavens and set the world spinning can be trusted, and no matter how difficult or confusing life gets, everything will come out right. With the Wisdom of Solomon *and* the whimsy of Pan, your greatest gift lies in your belief and optimism *and your ability to infuse others with it*. You could sell snow to Eskimos, turn sinners into saints, write a best-selling novel, teach, or scale Mt. Everest. As the cheerleader of the zodiac you can easily inspire others in any field you choose. Sagittarians like Walt Disney, Arthur C. Clarke, Steven Spielberg, and Brad Pitt show the variety of exciting career choices for your talents and intellect.

CAPTURES THE

Sagittarian PHILOSOPHY:

"Man is what he believes."
~ *Anton Chekov*

~~~~~~~~~~~~~~~~~~~~~~~~~~~

Successful Sagittarians

Britney Spears, Julianne Moore, Steven Bochco, Anita Baker, Dale Carnegie, Tina Turner, Billy Idol, Jane Fonda, Benjamin Bratt, Bette Midler, Brendon Fraser, Jane Austen, Kim Basinger, Frank Sinatra, Ludwig van Beethoven, Billy Idol

Preferred Professions

Writer,
Lecturer, Diplomat,
Broadcaster, Motivational
Speaker, Firefighter, Nun,
Lawyer, Travel Agent, Editor,
Publisher, Promoter, Minister,
Publicist, Translator, Salesperson,
Explorer, Professor, Bookseller,
Importer, Exporter, Jockey,
Philosopher

Capricorn

...on the Road to Success

DECEMBER 22 ~ JANUARY 19

"Climb every mountain / Ford every stream / Follow every rainbow / Till you find your dream" could have been written for a Capricorn as well as the classic film *Sound of Music*. When it comes to success in work and career, your ambitious, dynamic nature will leave no stone unturned and no challenge unmet. In short, Capricorn, you are born and bred

"Where he falls short, 'tis Nature's fault alone. Where he succeeds, the merit's all his own." ~ *Charles Churchill*

Element: Earth
Quality: Cardinal
Ruler: Saturn
Symbol: Goat

Capricorn
COMPATIBLE
SIGNS

~*Earth Signs*
★ Taurus
★ Virgo
★ Capricorn

~*Water Signs*
★ Cancer
★ Scorpio
★ Pisces

to take your place as a captain of industry and pillar of society, among the movers and shakers of the world. Capricorns Aristotle Onassis and Howard Hughes exemplify some of the resourceful, financially astute qualities bestowed by your Saturn ruler.

Your magic lies in your innate executive, managerial skills and self-discipline, and suits you well for running a home, a company, or a country. You rise to the top with an uncanny knack to know how to accomplish your goals with an economy of effort and resources. The words *savvy, disciplined,* and *determined* aptly describe your personality and once you've set your mind to something, it's only a matter of time before you get the results you want. Wise beyond your years, your confidence increases with experience and age, a gift from your stern but rewarding ruler, Saturn.

CAPTURES THE

Capricorn PHILOSOPHY:

"To travel hopefully is a better thing than to arrive, and the true success is labor." ~ *Donald H. McGannon*

Successful Capricorns

Jude Law, Diane Sawyer, Jeff Bezos, Annie Lennox, Denzel Washington, Diane Keaton, Mel Gibson, Ricky Martin, Katie Couric, Matt Lauer, Nicolas Cage, Julia Ormand, Tiger Woods, Jim Carrey, Martin Luther King, Jr.

Preferred Professions

Builder,
Account Executive,
Astronomer, Dentist,
Economist, Engineer, Realtor,
Foreman, Geologist, Industrialist,
Mathematician, Mineralogist,
Mining Engineer, Musician, Stone
Cutter, Statesman, Proprietor,
Manager, Labor Leader,
Sculptor, Teacher

Aquarius
...on the Road to Success

JANUARY 20 ~ FEBRUARY 18

You could write the book on original-
ity and uniqueness, Aquarius,
thanks to Uranus, your unorthodox ruler.
Maybe that's why many Aquarians are
found in the Hall of Fame as notable
trailblazers, inventors, and noncon-
formists who do things *their way*. Being
different isn't easy, but Aquarians Oprah
Winfrey, Paul Newman, and Abraham

"If a man does not keep pace with his
companions, perhaps it is because he
hears a different drummer." ~ *Thoreau*

Element: Air
Quality: Fixed
Ruler: Uranus
Symbol: Water-
bearer

Aquarian
COMPATIBLE
SIGNS

~*Air Signs*
★ Gemini
★ Libra
★ Aquarius

~*Fire Signs*
★ Aries
★ Leo
★ Sagittarius

Lincoln prove how rewarding
and valuable it can be to
buck trends and set new standards. Celebrate your differ-
ence by cultivating your origi-
nality. You are not meant to
follow the crowd.

Your magic lies in your
inventive, unique view of the
world and your ability to shake
up the status quo from time
to time and keep progress in
motion. The price for being
unique isn't easy in youth but
gets easier as you age and
realize how rewarding it is to

"take the road less traveled by." You don't suffer fools gladly and are nobody's clone but you can work for large corporations that utilize your special talents and skills.

You're a great worker, friend, and humanitarian, with a myriad of talents to keep you active and interested your entire life. If you follow your heart and interests, your life will never be dull or ordinary, Aquarius.

CAPTURES THE *Aquarian* PHILOSOPHY:

"I did it my way."
~ *Song title and lyrics, Paul Anka*

∿∿∿∿∿∿∿∿∿∿∿∿∿∿∿

Successful Aquarians

Tom Brokaw, Jennifer Aniston, Nathan Lane, Rene Russo, John McEnroe, Michael Jordan, Brandy, Norman Rockwell, Bridget Fonda, Mozart, Baryshnikov, Charles Lindbergh, James Dean, Natalie Cole, Garth Brooks, John Travolta, Sarah McLachlan, Thomas Edison

Preferred Professions

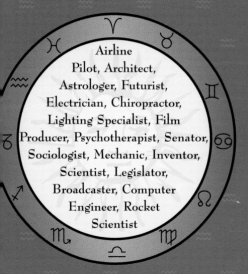

Airline
Pilot, Architect,
Astrologer, Futurist,
Electrician, Chiropractor,
Lighting Specialist, Film
Producer, Psychotherapist, Senator,
Sociologist, Mechanic, Inventor,
Scientist, Legislator,
Broadcaster, Computer
Engineer, Rocket
Scientist

Pisces

...on the Road to Success

FEBRUARY 19 ~ MARCH 20

The imaginative, gentle, Pisces qualities you possess, bestowed by Neptune, your ruler, can easily be expressed in a variety of careers and work that call for inspiration and intuition. Kindhearted, sympathetic, and sensitive by nature, you still have what it takes to succeed in today's world, and you can *excel* in jobs and careers that capitalize on your abilities and talents.

"We are such stuff as dreams are made on." ~ The Tempest, *Shakespeare*

Element: Water
Quality: Mutable
Ruler: Neptune
Symbol: Fish

Pisces
COMPATIBLE
SIGNS

~*Water Signs*
★ Cancer
★ Scorpio
★ Pisces

~*Earth Signs*
★ Taurus
★ Virgo
★ Capricorn

Consider the variety of careers that express Pisces' talents through the imaginative humor of Billy Crystal, the corporate visionary skills of Michael Eisner, and the music of Chopin. They demonstrate how effectively and diversely your Pisces imagination and sensitivity can serve you, personally and professionally. What you dream you can create, a desirable and lucrative asset for a profession or job in film, music, art, in marketing, promotions, or in any work or profession that requires creativity and vision.

Your magic lies in your sensitivity, imagination, and intuition. You are the dream weaver, the hypnotist, the taleteller, actor, artist, visionary, and most spiritual sign of the zodiac. Is it any wonder that when you come from your finest qualities and great talents, Pisces, you're the best chance we have for a glimpse into heaven?

CAPTURES THE

Pisces PHILOSOPHY:

"A Dream Is a Wish Your Heart Makes" ~ *Song title and lyric*, Cinderella

~~~~~~~~~~~~~~~~~~~~~~~~

Successful Pisceans

Sharon Stone, David Geffen, Bruce Willis, Drew Barrymore, Steve Jobs, Vanessa Williams, George Washington, Cindy Crawford, Ansel Adams, Juliette Binoche, Holly Hunter, Rob Lowe, Miranda Richardson, Quincy Jones, Glenn Close, Liz Taylor, Albert Einstein

Preferred Professions

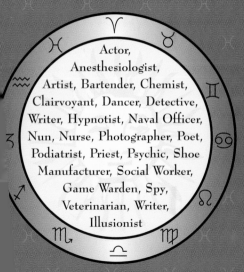

Actor, Anesthesiologist, Artist, Bartender, Chemist, Clairvoyant, Dancer, Detective, Writer, Hypnotist, Naval Officer, Nun, Nurse, Photographer, Poet, Podiatrist, Priest, Psychic, Shoe Manufacturer, Social Worker, Game Warden, Spy, Veterinarian, Writer, Illusionist

Lee Holloway is an internationally published author, astrologer, and broadcaster. A Sagittarius and mother of three, she lives in Woodland Hills, California.